# QUICK MEALS

## Ready in 30 Minutes or Less

### Kathy Berget

# MEAT TEMPERATURE CHART

Rare 120-125°F
Medium Rare 130-135°F
Medium 140-145°F
Medium Well 150-155°F
Well Done 160°F

White Meat 165°F
Dark Meat 185°F

145°F

145°F

(Salmon
Medium Rare 120°F-130°F
Well Done 145°F )

# To My Family

You are my inspiration!

# Tips for 30-Minute Meals

## Plan Your Week

- Knowing what you'll cook daily prevents last-minute scrambles and saves time at the grocery store. Make a menu and write it down. It's okay if it changes, but having a plan helps!

## Read the Entire Recipe

- Before starting, read through the entire recipe. Make certain you have all the ingredients and just before cooking, place all ingredients on the counter where you'll be preparing your meal.

## Organize Your Kitchen

- Keep your kitchen essentials (knives, cutting boards, pots, and pans) in easy-to-reach places. A well-organized kitchen makes moving quickly and efficiently through a recipe easier.

## Use Your Pantry

- Keep versatile pantry staples (like pasta, rice, and canned goods) on hand for fast, easy meals. A well-stocked pantry allows you to whip up meals without frequent grocery trips.

## Keep it Simple

- Focus on recipes with fewer ingredients and straightforward techniques. Simplicity allows the flavors of each component to shine and ensures you can cook quickly without getting overwhelmed.

## Multitask

- While one element of the meal is cooking, use that time to prep or cook another component. Multitasking ensures you're using your time efficiently.

## Preheat and Pre-Boil

- Start boiling water or preheating your oven as soon as you begin prepping, so everything is ready when needed.

## Utilize Quick-Cooking Proteins

- Opt for proteins that cook quickly, such as shrimp, fish, chicken breast, or eggs. Thin cuts of meat or ground meats also cook faster and can be flavored in various ways.

## Use Prepared Ingredients

- Foods like pre-washed greens, canned beans, or rotisserie chicken are excellent time savers. These let you skip lengthy prep work without compromising the quality of your meals.

## Cook in Batches

- Cook larger portions of grains, sauces, or proteins ahead of time and store them in the fridge or freezer. These can be quickly transformed into different meals throughout the week.

## Clean as You Go

- While you're waiting for something to cook or simmer, tidy up the kitchen. This helps keep your workspace organized and reduces cleanup after cooking.

# Bruschetta Chicken

*Thinly sliced chicken breasts and a fresh tomato and basil topping make a fresh tasting light dinner. The bruschetta topping is delicious served with crispy French bread too!*

## Ingredients

- 2 boneless, skinless chicken breasts, sliced in half horizontally into thin fillets
- 1/2 teaspoon salt
- 1/4 teaspoon pepper
- 1/4 teaspoon garlic powder
- 1 tablespoon olive oil

- 1 1/2 cups chopped tomatoes
- 1/4 cup chopped white onion
- 4-5 basil leaves cut into thin strips
- 1 tablespoon balsamic vinegar

## Instructions

1. Dry chicken fillets by patting with a paper towel.
2. Sprinkle with salt, pepper, and garlic powder.
3. Heat oil in a pan over medium to medium-high heat. When hot, but not smoking, add fillets and cook on each side for 3-4 minutes until browned and fully cooked and reaches at least 165°F. If needed, cook for an additional 1-2 minutes per side.
4. While the chicken is cooking, combine chopped tomatoes, onions, basil, and balsamic vinegar.
5. Place cooked chicken breasts on a serving platter. Place a spoonful of tomato mixture on the top of each breast.
6. Serve hot with extra tomato mixture on the side.

- If the chicken sticks to the pan when you go to flip it, give it another 30-60 seconds and try again. It will naturally release from the pan when it's ready to be flipped.
- Try the tomato bruschetta mixture and add salt and pepper if desired.
- A sprinkling of Parmesan cheese can be added just before serving

# Panko Chicken

*Crispy panko breadcrumbs add extra crunch to lightly fried chicken cutlets. Serve with potatoes and gravy or slice into thin strips and add to a salad.*

## Ingredients

- 2 boneless, skinless chicken breasts, sliced in half horizontally into thin fillets
- 1 teaspoon salt
- 2 eggs
- 1 1/2 cups panko breadcrumbs
- 1/2 cup flour
- 1 teaspoon Italian seasoning
- 1/2 teaspoon pepper
- 1/4 teaspoon garlic powder
- 1/4 teaspoon paprika
- 3 tablespoons oil (olive, canola, vegetable, or your favorite cooking oil)
- Chopped parsley for garnish, optional

## Instructions

1. Pat chicken breasts dry with a paper towel and sprinkle both sides of chicken with salt.
2. In a large flat bowl, beat the eggs with a fork so the yolk and whites are combined.
3. In a separate large flat bowl, combine panko, flour, Italian seasoning, pepper, garlic powder, and paprika.
4. Heat a large skillet over medium heat with the oil.
5. Dredge each piece of chicken into the egg and then into the panko mixture. Pat the mixture firmly onto both sides of the chicken. Set aside and continue with remaining pieces.
6. Place chicken in hot pan and cook for 4-5 minutes per side until golden. Flip and cook the other side until the chicken is cooked and reaches at least 165°F.
7. Serve hot garnished with freshly chopped parsley.

- Don't overcrowd pan while cooking. If needed, use two pans or cook in two batches.
- Try to flip only once.
- If your chicken browns too quickly in the pan but isn't fully cooked, transfer to a baking sheet lined with a baking rack and place in a preheated 350°F oven for 5-10 minutes to finish cooking. This helps keep the chicken juicy and ensures it's cooked through.

# Parmesan Chicken Pasta

*A delicious one pot meal with the pasta cooked right in the sauce. Leftovers are just as delicious the next day too!*

## Ingredients

- 2 chicken breasts, boneless skinless, cut into 1-2 inch cubes
- 2 tablespoons olive oil
- 1/2 teaspoon salt
- 1/4 teaspoon pepper
- 1/4 teaspoon garlic powder
- 3 cups marinara sauce (1 24-ounce jar)
- 3 cups water
- 1 teaspoon Italian seasoning
- 1 pound uncooked rigatoni pasta or ziti pasta
- 1/2 cup shredded mozzarella cheese
- 1/2 cup shredded Parmesan cheese
- Fresh parsley or basil for garnish

## Instructions

1. Season chicken with garlic powder, salt, and pepper.
2. Heat a deep skillet or large pot over medium heat. Add olive oil and then add chicken. Cook without stirring for 3-5 minutes until browned.
3. Flip chicken and cook other side until browned. If the chicken sticks to the pan, give it another 30-60 seconds and try again.
4. Remove from pan and set aside. The chicken will not be fully cooked.
5. Add marinara sauce, water, and Italian seasoning. Scrape up any bits from the bottom of the pan. Turn heat to high and bring to a boil.
6. When the sauce begins to boil, add uncooked pasta and stir well. Place a lid on pan and reduce heat. Stir pasta once or twice while cooking. Cook until the pasta is cooked to your liking.
7. Add chicken back into the sauce.
8. Add half the mozzarella cheese and half the Parmesan cheese. Stir and simmer for 1-2 minutes until the chicken is fully cooked, 165°F.
9. Remove from heat and sprinkle with remaining cheese and chopped parsley or basil for garnish.
10. Serve hot.

- Use your favorite variety of pasta.
- Taste the pasta to determine when it's done to your liking.
- For a different taste, use bulk Italian sausage instead of the chicken. Be certain to strain off any remaining grease after browning the sausage.

# Grilled Chicken Legs

*Perfectly seasoned chicken legs with crispy skin cooked outdoors on the grill.*

## Ingredients

- **8 chicken legs**
- **2 tablespoons olive oil**
- **2 teaspoons salt**
- **1 teaspoon pepper**
- **1 teaspoon garlic powder**
- **1 teaspoon onion powder**
- **1 teaspoon dried thyme leaves**
- **1 teaspoon smoked paprika or regular paprika**

## Instructions

1. Preheat grill to **415-450°F.**
2. Scrape grates and apply a small amount of oil across the top of the grates to help prevent sticking. (Fold a paper towel and dip lightly into cooking oil. Use tongs to grab the paper towel and rub over the grates.)
3. Pat chicken legs dry with a paper towel.
4. Place in a large zip-top bag.
5. Add olive oil. Seal bag and rotate chicken so the olive oil coats all areas.
6. Combine seasoning and add to the bag. Reseal and rotate so the seasoning is well distributed.
7. Place legs on hot grill and cook over medium heat with the lid closed for **4-5 minutes per side.** Rotate every **5 minutes** until the legs are fully cooked and reach at least **185°F.**
8. Remove from grill and let rest for **5 minutes** before serving.

- Chicken is fully cooked when the internal temperature reaches 165°F. However, legs benefit from extra cooking time because it helps make them more tender.
- This recipe can also be cooked in an oven. Bake in a preheated **415°F** oven for **30-35 minutes** until the chicken is baked through and reaches an internal temperature of **185°F.** No need to flip chicken while it's baking.

# Lemon Chicken

*This lemon chicken takes a few extra steps, but the results are ultra delicious. Serve with pasta, mashed potatoes or rice.*

## Ingredients

- 2 boneless, skinless chicken breasts, sliced in half horizontally into thin fillets
- 1/2 teaspoon salt
- 1/4 teaspoon pepper
- 1/3 cup flour
- 2 tablespoons butter
- 1 tablespoon olive oil

Sauce
- 1 tablespoon olive oil, if needed
- 2 tablespoons finely chopped shallots
- 1 teaspoon finely chopped garlic
- 1/2 cup white wine, pinot grigio or chardonnay
- 1/2 cup chicken broth
- Zest from 1 lemon
- 2 tablespoons lemon juice
- 1 tablespoon fresh parsley, chopped
- Lemon slices, garnish
- Fresh parsley, chopped for garnish

## Instructions

1. Sprinkle both sides of chicken with salt and pepper
2. Dredge the breasts, one at a time in the flour coating both sides. Shake off any excess flour.
3. Heat a large skillet over medium heat. Add butter and one tablespoon of olive oil. When oil is shimmering, add the chicken breasts. Adjust heat to medium-low.
4. Cook for 4-5 minutes until golden. Flip chicken and cook for another 4-5 minutes until golden and cooked through, at least 165°F. Remove chicken from the pan and set aside.
5. Turn heat to low. If the pan is dry, add an additional tablespoon of olive oil to the pan. Cook shallots for 1-2 minutes until they begin to soften. Add garlic and cook for about 30 seconds until the garlic becomes fragrant.
6. Add the wine to the pan. Turn the heat to medium. Use a silicone spatula or a wooden spoon to scrape up all the browned bits from the bottom of the pan. Simmer to reduce wine to half.
7. Add chicken stock and heat until simmering.
8. Return chicken breasts back to pan along with any juices that accumulated on the plate. Cook for 2-3 minutes.
9. Turn off heat. Stir in lemon zest, lemon juice and parsley.
10. Serve hot with extra sauce spooned over the top of the chicken. Add lemon slices and extra parsley for garnish.

# Creamy Chicken Orzo

*Tender chicken strips, creamy orzo pasta, and fresh spinach come together in a rich, flavorful dish. Bursting with garlic, tomatoes, and fresh basil flavors, it's a comforting meal that's both hearty and delicious.*

## Ingredients

- 1 1/2 pounds boneless, skinless chicken breasts, cut into 1-inch strips
- 1 tablespoon olive oil
- 1/4 teaspoon garlic powder
- 1/4 teaspoon Italian seasoning
- 1/4 teaspoon salt
- 1/4 teaspoon pepper

- 1 1/4 cups uncooked orzo pasta
- 1 tablespoon olive oil
- 2 teaspoons garlic, minced
- 2 1/2 cups chicken broth
- 1/4 teaspoon salt
- 1 cup heavy cream
  2 cups baby spinach
- 1 cup grape tomatoes, halved
- 1 tablespoon fresh basil, chopped

## Instructions

1. Sprinkle chicken with salt, pepper, garlic powder, and Italian seasoning.
2. Place oil in a pan over medium heat. When the oil is shimmering, add sliced chicken. Cook for 3-4 minutes per side until browned. Remove from pan and set aside. The chicken will not be fully cooked.
3. Turn the heat to low and add another tablespoon of oil. Add uncooked orzo and stir to coat. Clear a space in the center of the pan and add garlic. Cook for about 30 seconds, stirring once or twice.
4. Add chicken broth and 1/4 teaspoon of salt. Stir, scrapping up any browned bits from the bottom of the pan. Turn heat to high and allow the mixture to boil until the orzo is almost cooked, stirring several times.
5. When most of the broth has been absorbed, turn heat to low and stir in heavy cream. Bring to a simmer, then return the browned chicken and any accumulated juices to the pan. Cook until the sauce has thickened and the orzo is soft and the chicken is cooked to at least 165°F. If the mixture becomes too thick, add 1-2 tablespoons of chicken broth.
6. Taste sauce and add additional salt and pepper, if needed.
7. Remove from heat and stir in the spinach, cherry tomatoes, and fresh basil.
8. Rest for 2-3 minutes and then stir again before serving.
9. Serve hot with fresh basil as a garnish.

# Baked Chicken Tacos

*Delicious tacos that are already assembled and ready to serve. Perfect for family meals or for game day.*

## Ingredients

- 2 cups cooked shredded chicken
- 1/2 cup onion, chopped
- 1 tablespoon oil (olive, vegetable, canola, or your favorite oil)
- 14.5-ounce can of diced tomatoes, drained
- 1 tablespoon chili powder
- 1 teaspoon ground cumin
- 1/2 teaspoon paprika
- 1/4 teaspoon garlic powder
- 1/4 teaspoon dried oregano
- 1/2 teaspoon salt
- 1/4 teaspoon pepper
- 15 ounce can black beans, rinsed and drained
- 10 taco shells, flat bottomed
- 2 cups shredded cheddar cheese
- Chopped tomatoes and fresh cilantro leaves for garnish.

## Instructions

1. Preheat oven to 400°F
2. Heat oil in a skillet over medium heat. Add onions and cook for 2-3 minutes, until onions begin to soften. Add drained tomatoes, and seasoning. Stir until combined. Add shredded chicken and cook until heated.
3. Place empty taco shells in a 9x13 casserole dish. Heat in oven for 2-3 minutes, until the shells are warmed. Remove from oven.
4. Add a layer of cheese to the bottom of each taco shell.
5. Spoon in a layer of beans and then a layer of the chicken mixture.
6. Top with additional cheese.
7. Place uncovered casserole dish in preheated oven for 7-10 minutes until the cheese is melted.
8. Serve hot, topped with freshly chopped cilantro and tomatoes.

- Can also be served with fresh salsa, sour cream, guacamole, crunchy lettuce and sliced jalapenos.

# BBQ Chicken Pizza

*Plan ahead and save some leftover chicken for this pizza. Serve with a dinner salad for a light meal or serve as an appetizer.*

## Ingredients

- 1 cup shredded chicken, fully cooked
- 2 Naan flatbreads, about 6x8 inches each
- 1/2 cup BBQ sauce, divided
- 1/2 cup mozzarella cheese
- 1/4 cup sliced red onion
- Sprinkle of fresh Parmesan cheese

## Instructions

1. Preheat oven to 425°F.
2. Place the flatbread on a baking sheet.
3. Combine 1/4 cup of the BBQ sauce with the shredded chicken.
4. Use the remaining 1/4 cup of BBQ sauce to spread over the top of each flatbread.
5. Sprinkle mozzarella over the sauce, and then top with shredded chicken and sliced onion.
6. Add Parmesan.
7. Bake in preheated oven for 12-15 minutes until heated.
8. Serve hot.

- Finely chopped pineapple is perfect for adding to this pizza. Sprinkle with a few small chunks before baking.
- If Naan flatbread isn't available, look for other flatbread that is sometimes available in your deli area or the bread aisle.

# Salsa Chicken

*Juicy chicken breasts are seasoned and seared to perfection, then topped with zesty salsa and melted pepper jack cheese. Use your favorite type of salsa and select hot, medium, or mild salsa to suit your taste.*

## Ingredients

- 4 chicken breasts, boneless and skinless
- 1/4 teaspoon salt
- 1/4 teaspoon pepper
- 1 tablespoon oil (olive, vegetable, canola, or your favorite cooking oil)
- 1 cup salsa
- 1/2 cup shredded pepper jack cheese or Monterey jack cheese
- Fresh cilantro for garnish, optional

## Instructions

1. Preheat oven to 415°F.
2. Place a tablespoon of oil in a large oven-safe skillet over medium heat.
3. Pat chicken breasts dry and sprinkle with salt and pepper.
4. Place in skillet and cook for 5-6 minutes on medium to medium-high heat until browned.
5. While the chicken is browning, heat salsa in the microwave for 60-90 seconds.
6. Flip chicken. Add hot salsa and top with shredded cheese.
7. Place skillet in preheated oven and cook until the chicken is fully cooked and has reached at least 165°F, for about 20-22 minutes.
8. Remove skillet from oven and serve hot topped with fresh cilantro for garnish.

- Actual cooking time will vary depending on the thickness of your chicken breasts.
- If your chicken breasts seem very large or you want the chicken to cook quicker, cut the breasts in half through the center to create two thin fillets.
- If skillet becomes dry while baking, add an additional 1/2 cup of hot salsa to pan.

# Ground Beef Stroganoff

*A classic dish made with ground beef instead of cubed beef. Use lean ground beef or use ground wild game like venison or elk.*

## Ingredients

- 1 pound lean ground beef
- 1 tablespoon olive oil
- 8 ounces mushrooms, sliced
- 1 small onion, diced
- 1 teaspoon garlic, finely diced
- 3 tablespoons flour
- 2 cups beef broth
- 1 tablespoon Worcestershire sauce
- 1 teaspoon Dijon mustard
- 1 teaspoon dried parsley
- 1/4 teaspoon dried thyme
- 1/4 teaspoon salt
- 1/8 teaspoon pepper
- 1/2 cup sour cream
- 8 ounces egg noodles
- Freshly chopped parsley for garnish, optional

## Instructions

1. Start a pot of water to boil for the noodles. When boiling, add noodles and cook to your liking.
2. While water is boiling, heat olive oil in a pan over medium heat.
3. Add mushrooms and cook for 5-6 minutes until browned. Remove mushrooms from pan. Set aside.
4. Add ground beef and stir to break up into large chunks. Once it is browned, push meat to one side of the pan. Drain any grease if needed. Add the onions to the other side of the pan. Cook for 1-2 minutes.
5. Add garlic and cook for about 30 seconds and then add flour. Combine everything in the pan and cook for one minute.
6. Slowly stir in beef broth. Add Worcestershire sauce, mustard, parsley, thyme, salt, and pepper.
7. Cook until the mixture begins to simmer and thicken. Simmer for 1-2 additional minutes.
8. Turn heat off and let mixture cool until it stops bubbling. Stir in sour cream.
9. Drain noodles. Serve stroganoff over noodles. Top with freshly chopped parsley.

- Drain off any excess grease after the burger has browned.
- Don't add the sour cream when the mixture is still bubbling. The sour cream may break or separate if it's too hot.
- Add additional salt, if needed.
- Can also be served over mashed potatoes or polenta.

# Chicken Fried Steak

*Every time I make this dish, I have to tell my husband it's not chicken, it's steak! I guess maybe I should rename it breaded cube steak.*

## Ingredients

- 1 pound cube steak, cut into 4 cube steaks
- 1/2 teaspoon salt
- 1 egg
- 1/3 cup milk
- 1 cup flour
- 1/2 teaspoon pepper
- 1/2 teaspoon paprika
- 1/4 teaspoon garlic powder
- 1/4 teaspoon onion powder
- 1/4 cup of oil for frying (vegetable, canola, or your favorite oil)

Gravy
- 1/4 cup flour
- 1-2 tablespoons of oil
- 2 cups whole milk
- 1/2 teaspoon salt
- 1/2 teaspoon pepper

## Instructions

1. Preheat oven to 200°F.
2. Sprinkle cube steaks with salt.
3. In a large shallow bowl combine egg and 1/3 cup of milk with a fork.
4. In another bowl combine flour, paprika, pepper, garlic powder, and onion powder.
5. Dip each steak into the egg mixture and then into the flour mixture. Press the steaks in the flour so both sides are fully covered. Place on a plate and continue with the remaining cube steaks.
6. Place 1/4 cup of oil in a large pan over medium heat.
7. Once the oil is hot, but not smoking, place the cube steaks in the pan. Cook over medium heat until golden brown, about 5 minutes. Flip and cook the other side for about 5 minutes. Turn off heat.
8. Remove cube steaks from pan and place on a baking rack over a cooking sheet and place in preheated oven. This will keep the cube steaks warm while you make the gravy.
9. Using the same pan over low heat, whisk in 1/4 cup of flour into any remaining oil in the pan. Add 1-2 additional tablespoons of oil until the flour is completely coated with oil. It can be thick, but you don't want any dry parts. Stir for one minute.
10. Slowly whisk in milk. Turn heat up to medium. Stir in 1/2 teaspoon salt and pepper. Whisk until it begins to simmer and thicken. Taste and add more salt if needed.
11. Serve cube steaks hot. Ladle gravy over each cube steak just before eating.

# Broccoli Beef

*Tender strips of sirloin steak and crisp broccoli are coated in a savory-sweet sauce with hints of garlic, ginger, and honey. This quick stir-fry delivers bold flavors in every bite.*

## Ingredients

- 1 pound top sirloin steak
- 1 head of broccoli, about 1 pound cut into small florets
- 2 tablespoons oil (olive, vegetable or your favorite oil)

Sauce
- 1/2 cup soy sauce, low-sodium
- 2 tablespoons cornstarch
- 2 teaspoons fresh garlic, minced
- 1/2 cup chicken broth
- 1 teaspoon sesame oil
- 2 teaspoons rice vinegar
- 2 tablespoons honey
- 1 teaspoon fresh ginger, grated
- Pinch red pepper flakes
- Sesame seeds for garnish, optional

## Instructions

1. Slice beef into very thin pieces.
2. Combine all the sauce ingredients in a bowl and whisk together.
3. Place a tablespoon of oil in a large pan over medium-high heat. Add the broccoli and cook for 5-7 minutes until the broccoli is vibrant in color and slightly softened.
4. Transfer broccoli to a bowl and set aside.
5. Add 1 tablespoon of oil to pan and add the sliced steak. Cook stirring often until browned, about 3-4 minutes.
6. Push all the meat to one side and then pour the prepared sauce into the pan. Stir together with the meat and scrape up all the brown bits from the pan.
7. Cook for 1-2 minutes until the sauce thickens. Return broccoli to the pan and stir until coated.
8. Transfer to a serving platter and sprinkle with sesame seeds.

- Serve over hot rice or noodles.
- Use low-sodium soy sauce so the dish doesn't taste too salty. If using regular soy sauce, reduce to 1/4 cup and mix with 1/4 cup of water.

# Pepper Beef

*A savory stir-fry with tender beef, vibrant bell peppers, and a flavorful soy-garlic sauce. Simple yet packed with bold flavors, it's a perfect go-to meal for any night of the week.*

## Ingredients

- 1 pound flank steak, cut into thin strips
- 2 tablespoons olive oil
- 1 red bell pepper, sliced
- 1 green bell pepper, sliced
- 1 small onion, sliced into strips
- 1 teaspoon garlic, minced
- 1/4 teaspoon ginger powder
- 1/4 cup soy sauce, low sodium
- 1 tablespoon brown sugar
- Pinch red pepper flakes, optional
- 4 teaspoons cornstarch
- 1/2 cup water
- 2 green onions, chopped

## Instructions

1. Place 1 tablespoon of olive oil in a large skillet over medium heat. Add peppers and onions and cook for 4-5 minutes until softened. Remove from skillet and set aside.
2. Add another tablespoon of olive oil to pan and then add sliced steak. Cook for 3-4 minutes before turning. If meat sticks to the bottom, give it another 30 seconds until it releases from the pan. Cook for another 2-3 minutes.
3. Combine garlic, ginger, soy sauce, brown sugar, and red pepper flakes in a bowl. Add to the pan with the steak and stir. Return peppers and onions to the pan.
4. Combine cornstarch and water in a small bowl. Mix until smooth. Add to the pan and stir until combined. Cook until the mixture comes to a simmer and the sauce thickens. If the sauce becomes too thick, add 2-3 tablespoons of water until desired consistency.
5. Remove from heat and add chopped green onions for garnish. Serve hot.

- Feel free to use all red peppers or other colored peppers.
- Sirloin or round steak can also be used in place of the flank steak.

# Ground Beef Lettuce Wraps

*Savory ground beef mixed with vegetables, hoisin, and soy sauce wrapped in crisp butter lettuce leaves for a fresh and flavorful bite.*

## Ingredients

- 1 pound lean ground beef
- 1/2 cup finely chopped white onion
- 1/4 cup finely chopped red bell pepper
- 8 ounce can water chestnuts, drained and finely chopped
- 8 green onions, chopped

Sauce
- 1/3 cup hoisin sauce
- 2 tablespoons soy sauce, low sodium
- 2 tablespoons rice vinegar
- 2 teaspoons sesame oil
- 1 teaspoon ground ginger
- 1 teaspoon finely minced garlic
- Pinch red pepper flakes

- 1 head butter lettuce, leaves removed, rinsed and dried

## Instructions

1. Heat a large skillet over medium-high heat. Add ground beef and stir to break up large chunks. Cook for 4-5 minutes until meat is browned.
2. Push meat to half of the pan. Drain grease, if needed. Add onions and peppers to the other half of the pan. Cook for 3-4 minutes until softened, stirring every few minutes. Mix ground beef, onions, and peppers together and stir in chestnuts.
3. In a bowl, combine hoisin, soy sauce, vinegar, sesame oil, ginger, garlic, and red pepper flakes. Pour over ground beef mixture in the pan. Stir to combine.
4. Remove pan from heat and stir in green onions.
5. Serve spooned onto lettuce leaves.

- You can also use iceberg or romaine lettuce.

# Sweet & Sour Meatballs

*Juicy meatballs, bell peppers, and pineapple chunks coated in a tangy homemade sweet and sour sauce.*

## Ingredients

- 25 fully cooked frozen meatballs, about 1 pound
- 2 bell peppers, chopped into chunks
- 1 cup pineapple chunks, drained (save juice for sauce)

Sauce
- 1 cup pineapple juice
- 3/4 cup brown sugar
- 1/2 cup water
- 1/3 cup rice wine vinegar
- 3 tablespoons ketchup
- 1 tablespoon soy sauce, low-sodium
- Pinch red pepper flakes, optional
- 1 1/2 tablespoons cornstarch mixed with 2 tablespoons water
- Chopped scallions or chives for garnish

## Instructions

1. In a large saucepan with a lid, stir together pineapple juice, brown sugar, vinegar, ketchup, soy sauce, red pepper flakes, and water. Cook over medium heat.
2. When the sauce begins to simmer, whisk in the cornstarch mixture.
3. Add frozen meatballs and chopped bell peppers.
4. Stir to coat and bring to a simmer. Cover the pan with a lid.
5. Turn heat to medium-low heat and cook for 8-10 minutes until the meatballs are fully heated.
6. Remove the lid and stir in pineapple chunks
7. Top with scallions or chopped chives for garnish.
8. Serve hot over rice or noodles.

- Use any type of fully-cooked meatballs. Do not thaw before using.
- Add additional veggies as desired. Some ideas include frozen shelled edamame, fresh broccoli, and fresh sugar snap peas. Add at the same time you add the meatballs.

# French Bread Pizza

*Crispy French bread topped with marinara, melted mozzarella, and your favorite pizza toppings. A simple, delicious pizza that's perfect for quick dinners or casual gatherings.*

## Ingredients

- 1 loaf French Bread
- 1 cup marinara sauce
- 1 1/2 cups shredded mozzarella cheese
- 1/4 cup pepperoni
- 1/2 sliced bell pepper
- 1/4 cup sliced mushrooms
- 1/4 cup grated Parmesan cheese

## Instructions

1. Preheat oven to 400°F.
2. Slice the bread in half lengthwise and place the cut side up on an ungreased baking sheet.
3. Place bread in oven for 5-7 minutes, until it begins to toast. The surface of the bread should feel slightly dry but it should not be browned.
4. Remove from oven and assemble pizzas.
5. Spread marinara sauce evenly over the cut half of the bread.
6. Sprinkle on mozzarella cheese and then add your choice of toppings.
7. Sprinkle Parmesan cheese over the top.
8. Return the pizzas to the oven and bake until the cheese is melted and the pizza is heated through about 10-12 minutes.
9. Remove from oven and let cool for 2-3 minutes before slicing and serving.

- Use your favorite pizza toppings - sliced black olives, salami, Canadian bacon, pineapple, or make it plain cheese.

# Creamy Sausage Pasta

*A rich and flavorful pasta dish featuring savory Italian sausage, fresh spinach, and sun-dried tomatoes in a creamy Parmesan sauce. Perfect for when you're craving a cozy, comforting meal that's ready in no time.*

## Ingredients

- 1 pound Italian sausage, hot or sweet
- 8 ounces penne pasta
- 1/2 cup chicken broth
- 1 1/2 cups heavy cream
- 1/2 teaspoon Italian seasoning
- 1/4 teaspoon garlic powder
- 1/4 teaspoon pepper
- 1 pinch red pepper flakes, optional
- 1 cup freshly grated Parmesan cheese
- 2 cups fresh baby spinach
- 1/4 cup chopped sun-dried tomatoes
- 1/4 teaspoon salt, if needed

## Instructions

1. Cook pasta according to package directions
2. Meanwhile, in a large pan, cook sausage until no longer pink. Remove sausage from pan and set aside. Wipe pan with a paper towel to remove excess grease.
3. Add broth to the pan and stir to deglaze the pan removing all the brown bits from the bottom of the pan.
4. Add cream, and seasonings and cook over medium-low heat until simmering, stirring occasionally.
5. Add Parmesan cheese. Stir until the cheese has melted.
6. Add sausage back into the pan along with the fresh spinach and sun-dried tomatoes. Cook until the spinach wilts.
7. Taste the sauce and add salt if desired.
8. Drain pasta and add to the sauce.
9. Stir so the pasta is fully coated. Simmer for 1-2 minutes.
10. Serve hot topped with additional Parmesan cheese and fresh herbs for garnish.

- Use bulk sausage or sausage links. If using links, remove the casing and break apart the sausage.
- Feel free to adjust the amount of red pepper flakes to your liking. Add more for a spicier dish or omit if you prefer a milder dish.

# 20 Minute Pork Chops

*Perfectly seasoned thin pork chops seared quickly for a flavorful meal in no time.*

## Ingredients

- **4 thin pork chops**
- **3/4 teaspoon salt**
- **1/2 teaspoon pepper**
- **1/4 teaspoon garlic powder**
- **1/4 teaspoon dried thyme**
- **1/4 teaspoon dried sage**
- **1 tablespoon butter**
- **1 tablespoon olive oil**
- **Freshly chopped parsley for garnish, optional**

## Instructions

1. Pat pork chops with a paper towel to remove excess moisture.
2. Combine seasoning.
3. Sprinkle both sides of the pork chops with mixed seasonings.
4. Heat butter and olive oil together in a large skillet over medium heat.
5. Place pork chops in pan and cook without moving the pork chops for about 5 minutes. Peek at the bottom of the chops, if golden, flip and cook for another 4-5 minutes until cooked to 145°F.
6. Remove from heat and place on a plate and cover loosely with foil. Let rest 5-10 minutes before serving.
7. Top with freshly chopped parsley.

- Cooking time will vary depending on the thickness of your pork chops and the pan you are using.
- If you'd like an easy sauce to pour over the pork chops, add 1-2 tablespoons of butter to the pan after the pork chops have been removed. Whisk the butter as it melts removing any brown bits from the surface of the pan. Drizzle over pork chops just before serving.

# Pork Tenderloin

*Juicy pork tenderloins seasoned with a blend of spices and roasted to perfection in just 30 minutes. This elegant dish proves that you don't need complex techniques to create a sophisticated meal.*

## Ingredients

- 2 pork tenderloins, about 1 pound each
- 1 tablespoon olive oil
- 1 teaspoon salt
- 1/2 teaspoon pepper
- 1/2 teaspoon garlic powder
- 1/2 teaspoon onion powder
- 1/2 teaspoon paprika
- 1/2 teaspoon dried thyme
- 1/2 teaspoon dried sage
- Fresh parsley or thyme, for garnish

## Instructions

1. Preheat oven to 425°F.
2. Remove any silverskin on the tenderloins. Silverskin is a silvery-thin membrane that may be connected to part of the tenderloin. If left on, it can be tough and chewy.
3. Pat tenderloins dry with a paper towel.
4. Rub olive oil over the tenderloins.
5. Sprinkle with salt.
6. Combine remaining seasoning in a bowl and then sprinkle over the tenderloins.
7. Heat a large ovenproof skillet over medium to medium-high heat. When hot, add the tenderloins and brown both sides for 2-3 minutes on each side. (I brown just the top and the bottom.)
8. Place the skillet with the tenderloins in the preheated oven and bake for 15-20 minutes until the center of each tenderloin reaches 140-145°F. The temperature will continue to rise while the meat rests.
9. Remove from the oven and tent lightly with foil and rest for 5-10 minutes.
10. Slice the tenderloins into medallions that are cut slightly at an angle.
11. Serve hot with a garnish of freshly chopped parsley or fresh thyme.

- Make certain you look for tenderloin and not a loin roast. Tenderloins are small, narrow, boneless cuts of meat. They are often sold two to a package.

# Italian Sausage Sandwich

*Savory Italian sausages sautéed with sweet bell peppers and onions and served on hoagie rolls makes a hearty and delicious sandwich.*

## Ingredients

- 5 Italian sausage links, hot or sweet
- 2 tablespoons olive oil
- 1 red bell pepper, sliced into thin strips
- 1 small white onion, sliced into thin strips

Sandwich
- 5 hoagie rolls
- 2 tablespoons olive oil
- 1 cup marinara sauce
- 1/3 cup shredded mozzarella cheese
- 1/3 cup shredded Parmesan cheese

## Instructions

1. Preheat oven to 375°F
2. Cook sausages in a skillet over medium heat, turning when each side becomes browned. Cook until sausages are fully cooked, at least 165°F.
3. While the sausages are cooking, heat 2 tablespoons of olive oil in a separate skillet. Add sliced peppers and onions. Cook until softened, about 8-10 minutes.
4. Slice the rolls in half, but not all the way through. Open the rolls and lay flat on a baking sheet with the inside of the rolls facing up.
5. Brush the rolls with olive oil and place in the oven for 4-5 minutes until they are slightly toasted. This helps prevent the buns from becoming soggy.
6. Once the sausages are fully cooked and the peppers and onions are done, assemble the sandwiches.
7. Spoon about 2 tablespoons of marinara sauce over the inside of the rolls.
8. Add sausage and add the remaining marinara sauce over the top of the sausage.
9. Top with mozzarella, peppers, onions, and then with Parmesan cheese.
10. Place in the oven for 3-4 minutes until the cheese is melted.
11. Serve hot.

# Creamy Tortellini Skillet

*Italian sausage combined with diced tomatoes, garlic, and tender cheese tortellini for a satisfying one-pot dish. This easy recipe is a comforting meal that comes together in no time.*

## Ingredients

- 1 pound Italian sausage, hot or sweet. If links, remove casings.
- 2 cloves minced garlic
- 3/4 cup heavy cream
- 1/2 cup chicken broth
- 14 ounce can diced tomatoes, with juice
- 1 pound cheese tortellini, fresh or frozen
- Pinch of red pepper flakes, optional
- 2 cups baby spinach, chopped into large pieces
- Freshly grated Parmesan cheese, optional

## Instructions

1. Cook Italian sausage in a large skillet over medium heat. Drain off any excess grease. Keep cooked sausage in the pan.
2. Add garlic and cook until fragrant, about 30 seconds.
3. Add heavy cream, chicken broth, and can of tomatoes with the juice.
4. Add tortellini and stir gently into the sauce. The tortellini will not all be submerged, but try to get them as flat as possible. Stir every few minutes rotating the tortellini.
5. Cook over medium heat until the sauce begins to simmer and thicken.
6. Test a tortellini. If it's tender, remove from the heat. Otherwise cook for another few minutes until tender.
7. Turn off heat and add the chopped spinach. Stir until the spinach is wilted.
8. Top with grated Parmesan and serve hot.

# Shrimp Scampi

*Sautéed shrimp cooked with garlic and finished with a splash of white wine and fresh lemon juice for a bright, flavorful dish. Quick and elegant, this recipe is perfect for a special occasion.*

## Ingredients

- 1 1/2 pounds thawed shrimp, peeled and deveined
- 2 tablespoons olive oil
- 1 tablespoon butter
- 3 teaspoons garlic, minced
- 1/2 cup dry white wine, chardonnay or pinot grigio
- 2 tablespoons freshly squeezed lemon juice
- 1 tablespoon butter
- 1/4 cup fresh parsley, finely chopped
- 1/8 teaspoon red pepper flakes
- Salt and pepper to taste
- Lemon slices for garnish

## Instructions

1. Heat a large skillet over medium heat with olive oil and butter.
2. When the butter is melted, add the shrimp. Cook for 1-2 minutes then flip and cook for 1-2 more minutes until shrimp turns pink.
3. Remove shrimp from pan and set aside.
4. Add wine and turn heat to high and cook until the wine has reduced by about half.
5. Add shrimp back to the pan. Stir to coat shrimp.
6. Turn off heat. Add lemon juice, remaining butter, red pepper flakes, and fresh parsley. Stir to combine.
7. Add salt and pepper if needed.
8. Serve hot with lemon slices.

- Shrimp is sold by a number that tells you how many shrimp are in a pound. A package that says 26/30 means you will get between 26 and 30 shrimp per pound. The higher the numbers, the smaller the shrimp. Any size shrimp works in this recipe.
- Thaw shrimp quickly by placing in a zip-top bag and submerging in cold water.

# Crispy Pan Fried Fish

*Coated in seasoned panko breadcrumbs, these fish fillets are lightly fried to crispy perfection.*

## Ingredients

- 4-5 fish fillets, skinless and boneless, 10-14 ounces total
- 1 egg
- 3/4 cup panko breadcrumbs
- 1/4 cup flour
- 1/2 teaspoon salt
- 1/2 teaspoon paprika
- 1/2 teaspoon Italian seasoning
- 1/4 teaspoon garlic powder
- 1/4 teaspoon pepper

- 1/3 cup of oil for frying (vegetable, canola, or your favorite oil)

## Instructions

1. Pat fish dry with a paper towel.
2. Beat egg in a shallow bowl.
3. In a separate bowl combine panko, flour, and seasonings.
4. Place a large pan over medium heat. Add 1/3 cup of oil to pan.
5. Working with one fillet at a time, dip into egg and then into panko mixture. Press fillets firmly into panko so they are well coated.
6. When oil is hot, but not smoking, place fish into pan and cook for 3-4 minutes until golden brown. Flip fish and cook other side until golden and the fish is fully cooked, 145°F.

- Use any type of thin, mild-tasting fish fillets. Some options include walleye, whitefish, tilapia, cod, or flounder.
- Cooking time will vary depending on the thickness of the fillets.

# Sheet Pan Shrimp

*Zesty shrimp seasoned with lemon, garlic, and spices, roasted to perfection on a sheet pan for a quick and easy meal.*

## Ingredients

- 1 pound thawed shrimp, peeled and deveined with or without tails
- Juice from 1 lemon
- 2 tablespoons olive oil
- 1/4 teaspoon paprika
- 1/4 teaspoon red pepper flakes
- 1/4 teaspoon garlic powder
- 1/4 teaspoon Italian seasoning
- 1/4 teaspoon pepper
- Fresh parsley for garnish, optional
- Lemon wedges

## Instructions

1. Preheat oven to 400°F.
2. Pat shrimp dry with a paper towel and set aside.
3. Add lemon juice, olive oil, paprika, red pepper flakes, garlic powder, Italian seasoning, and pepper to a large mixing bowl. Mix until combined.
4. Add shrimp and toss until well-coated.
5. Place shrimp on a sheet pan and spread out in a single layer.
6. Place pan in oven and cook for 7-10 minutes until shrimp are pink.
7. Remove from oven and place on a serving dish. Sprinkle with freshly grated parsley and serve with lemon wedges.

- Shrimp is sold by a number that tells you how many shrimp are in a pound. A package that says 26/30 means you will get between 26 and 30 shrimp per pound. The higher the numbers, the smaller the shrimp. Any size shrimp works in this recipe.
- Thaw shrimp quickly by placing in a zip-top bag and submerging in cold water.

# Honey Garlic Salmon

*Pan-seared salmon fillets topped with a sweet and savory honey garlic sauce. Ready in just 20 minutes!*

## Ingredients

- **4 salmon fillets, skin-on**
- **1/4 teaspoon salt**
- **1 tablespoon olive oil**
- **1/4 cup honey**
- **2 tablespoons soy sauce, low sodium**
- **2 teaspoons minced garlic**
- **1 tablespoon lemon juice**
- **Freshly chopped chives**

## Instructions

1. Pat fish dry with paper towels.
2. Sprinkle the top of the fish with salt.
3. Combine honey, soy sauce, garlic, and lemon juice. Set aside.
4. Heat the oil in a large skillet over medium heat.
5. When pan is hot, add fish, skin-side up. Press down on the fish with a spatula to help ensure the fish has good contact with the pan. This helps with the browning and crispiness of the fish. Cook for **4-5 minutes** until golden brown.
6. Flip fish and continue cooking for **2-3 minutes** until the fish is cooked to your liking.
7. Pour sauce over the top of the fish. Cook for **1-2** minutes until the sauce has thickened and reduced by about half. Spoon the sauce over the fish while the sauce is reducing.
8. Remove fish from heat. Spoon any additional sauce over the top of each fillet.
9. Top with chopped chives for garnish.

- Test the fish with an instant-read thermometer inserted into the center of the fillet. 120°F-130°F is medium- rare and 145°F is well-done.
- The salmon can be served with the skin on or removed before serving. To remove, slide a thin metal spatula between the skin and the cooked fillet.
- Cooking time will vary depending on the thickness of the fillets.

# Bean Tostadas

*These tostadas start with quick but amazing refried beans that add an incredible amount of flavor.*

## Ingredients

- 1 tablespoon olive oil
- 1/2 teaspoon ground cumin
- 1/8  teaspoon smoked paprika
- 1/8 teaspoon chili powder
- 1/8 teaspoon garlic powder
- 15 ounce can pinto beans, do not drain

- 8 tostada shells
- 1 cup shredded cheddar cheese
- 1 cup finely chopped lettuce
- 1/2 cup chopped tomatoes
- 1/2 cup chopped avocado
- 1/4 cup chopped onions

## Instructions

1. Preheat oven to 250°F.
2. Heat the oil in a large skillet over low heat.
3. Add the spices and stir for 30 seconds until you can smell the spices.
4. Add the beans along with the sauce from the beans. Stir well and begin mashing the beans with a fork, a potato masher, or a large spoon. You want about 3/4 of the beans mashed.
5. Cook over low to medium-low heat until the beans have thickened.
6. Place tostada shells on a baking sheet and heat in the oven until warmed, about 5 minutes.
7. Top each shell with a spoonful of beans, then sprinkle with cheese, lettuce, tomatoes, onions, and avocado.

- Other topping ideas include salsa, hot sauce, sour cream, guacamole, or sliced olives.

# Pasta & Marinara

*This homemade marinara sauce can be used in so many recipes or ladled over spaghetti noodles for a classic dinner.*

## Ingredients

- 1 tablespoon olive oil
- 1 tablespoon garlic, minced
- 2 tablespoons tomato paste
- 28 ounce can of tomatoes, whole or diced
- 1/2 teaspoon dried oregano
- 1 teaspoon dried basil
- Pinch red pepper flakes
- 1/2 teaspoon sugar
- 1/4 - 1/2 teaspoon salt
- Fresh basil leaves for garnish

## Instructions

1. Heat olive oil in a saucepan over medium heat.
2. Add garlic and stir until fragrant, about 30 seconds.
3. Stir in tomato paste and dried oregano.
4. Add canned tomatoes along with the juice. Stir well until combined. If using whole tomatoes, smash tomatoes with the back of a wooden spoon until they are in small pieces.
5. Add basil and red pepper flakes.
6. Bring to a simmer and turn heat to medium-low. Cook for 20-25 minutes, stirring often so the bottom doesn't burn.
7. Add sugar and salt.
8. Turn heat to low and continue to simmer until ready to serve.
9. Serve over hot spaghetti or pasta noodles.

# Vegetarian Enchilada Skillet

*A hearty vegetarian enchilada skillet loaded with black beans, corn, bell peppers, and tortillas, all simmered in a flavorful enchilada sauce.*

## Ingredients

- 1 tablespoon olive oil
- 1/2 cup chopped onion
- 1/2 cup chopped red bell pepper
- 1 teaspoon garlic, minced
- 1/2 teaspoon cayenne pepper
- 1/2 teaspoon smoked paprika
- 1/2 teaspoon cumin powder
- 1/2 teaspoon dried oregano
- 1/4 teaspoon salt
- 1/4 teaspoon pepper
- 15 ounce can diced tomatoes, with juice
- 10 ounce can red enchilada sauce
- 15 ounce can black beans, rinsed and drained
- 1 cup frozen corn
- 4 ounce can diced green chiles, drained
- 6 white corn tortillas cut into ½ inch strips
- 1/2 cup shredded cheddar cheese
- 1/2 cup shredded pepper jack cheese

## Instructions

1. Heat oil in a large skillet over medium heat. Add onions and cook for 3-4 minutes.
2. Add red bell peppers and continue cooking for 2-3 minutes.
3. Add garlic, cayenne, smoked paprika, cumin, oregano, salt, and pepper. Stir until fragrant.
4. Stir in diced tomatoes, enchilada sauce, black beans, corn, and green chiles.
5. Bring to a simmer, then stir in tortilla strips.
6. Sprinkle cheese over the top. Place lid on pan and turn heat to low. Simmer for 5 minutes until cheese is melted.
7. Serve hot.

- Mixture can be served over hot rice or served with corn chips or warmed tortillas.
- Serve with sour cream, chopped avocados and fresh cilantro leaves.

# Frittata

*A frittata is similar to a giant omelet, but it's cooked first on the stovetop and then finished in the oven. No flipping needed! Serve for brunch or dinner.*

## Ingredients

- 1 tablespoon olive oil
- 8 eggs
- 1/2 cup milk
- 1/2 teaspoon salt
- 1/4 teaspoon pepper
- 1/8 teaspoon garlic powder
- 1/2 cup chopped tomatoes, use the meaty part of the tomatoes. Discard the seeds and excess juice.
- 1 cup baby spinach, coarsely chopped
- 1 cup shredded cheddar cheese

## Instructions

1. Preheat oven to 400°F.
2. Whisk together eggs, milk, salt, pepper, and garlic powder.
3. Fold in tomatoes, spinach, and 3/4 cup of cheese
4. Heat oil in a 10-12 inch cast iron skillet or heavy oven-safe skillet over medium heat.
5. Add egg mixture and cook over medium heat until the mixture becomes slightly bubbly and the edges are beginning to set.
6. Add remaining cheese to the top of the eggs and place pan in the preheated oven.
7. Bake for 12-18 minutes until the eggs are cooked on top and the frittata jiggles slightly when you shake the pan.
8. Allow frittata to rest for 5-10 minutes before slicing and serving.

- Cooking time will vary depending on the size of the pan you use.
- Feel free to add chopped ham, cooked bacon or cooked breakfast sausage to the egg mixture.
- Use your favorite type of cheese. Some options include Monterey Jack, smoked gouda or a sharp white cheddar.

# Green Chile Mac & Cheese

*Rich and creamy macaroni and cheese made with a blend of cheddar and Monterey jack, combined with roasted green chiles for a flavorful twist. This easy dish adds just the right amount of heat to classic comfort food.*

## Ingredients

- **8** ounces pasta, I used cellentani pasta. Can also use macaroni, penne or other hearty pasta.
- 1 teaspoon salt, for pasta water, optional
- 2 tablespoons butter
- 2 tablespoons flour
- 1/2 teaspoon dried mustard
- 1 1/2 cups milk
- 1 cup shredded cheddar cheese, about 2 1/2 ounces
- 1 cup shredded Monterey jack cheese, about 2 1/2 ounces
- 1/4 teaspoon salt
- 1/4 teaspoon pepper
- 1/2 cup diced roasted green chiles. If using canned, drain.

## Instructions

1. Bring a large pot of water to boil. Once boiling add a teaspoon of salt to the water and then add the pasta. Stir once or twice while cooking. Cook until al dente, or to your liking.
2. When cooked, drain well.
3. While the pasta is cooking, in a separate pot, heat butter over medium-low heat until melted. Whisk in flour and dried mustard. Cook for a minute while stirring.
4. Slowly whisk in milk. Turn heat up to medium. Whisk often until the milk thickens.
5. Remove from heat and slowly whisk in cheese.
6. Stir in diced chiles.
7. Pour drained pasta into cheese sauce. Stir well.
8. Allow the pasta to rest for about **5** minutes before serving.

# About the Author

Kathy is the creator of the blog, Beyond the Chicken Coop, where she is the recipe developer, food stylist and photographer. She started the blog in January 2015 as a hobby and it quickly grew into a passion and a full-time career. Beyond the Chicken Coop focuses on delicious homemade recipes with the occasional post about gardening, farm animals, and country living.

From an early age, Kathy has always had a love for cooking and baking. As a young teenager, she loved reading cookbooks and helping in the kitchen. She started planning and cooking dinners for her family when she was 13. While not all of those dishes were winners, Kathy learned how to cook, developed a love for cooking and learned how to hone her craft.

For 27 years, Kathy worked in elementary schools as a teacher and then as a school principal. Kathy loves cooking for her husband and their three children. They are her official taste testers and are still the ones Kathy loves cooking for today! Cooking has always been a way for her to relax and share her love.

This cookbook is a collection of recipes of delicious dinners perfect for any day of the week!

# Thank you!

Thanks to my husband, Rod who supports all of my crazy ideas! Thanks to my children, Taylor, Zachary, and Kristopher who inspire me in new ways every day and who eat all my kitchen creations!

A huge thank you to my mom, Judy for always supporting me and for being my editor in chief! I couldn't have done this cookbook without you!

Be certain to check out my other cookbook, Quick Breads - 30 delicious recipes!